Wonderful Wilderness

Written by Gill Arb

T0328009

Contents

Collins

What is a wilderness?

A wilderness is an **area** of land that hasn't been **significantly** changed by humans. Wildernesses are the last really wild places on Earth.

Until recent times, people only affected quite small areas of the planet, and most of the earth was wilderness. The wilderness was something to be afraid of, full of wild animals that could kill you, forests where you could become hopelessly lost, and icy mountains where you could fall to your death.

Amazon rainforest

Snowdonia

As human populations expanded and cities grew bigger, wild areas began to shrink. They also became busier, as people started to use wildernesses as places to enjoy themselves – for instance, going walking and climbing for pleasure.

Sahara desert

Many poets and painters also started to use the landscape to inspire their work. People began to realise that wilderness areas needed protection.

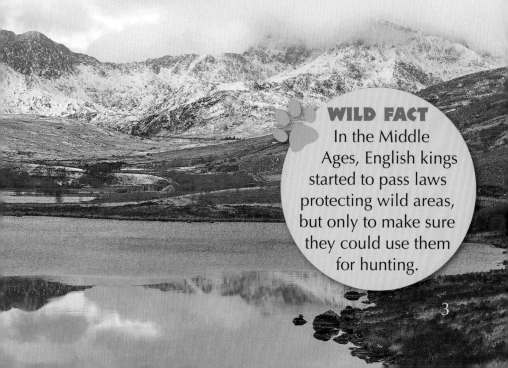

WILD FACT
In the Middle Ages, English kings started to pass laws protecting wild areas, but only to make sure they could use them for hunting.

3

Where in the world are the wildernesses?

There are wildernesses on every continent, but they're not evenly spread around the world.

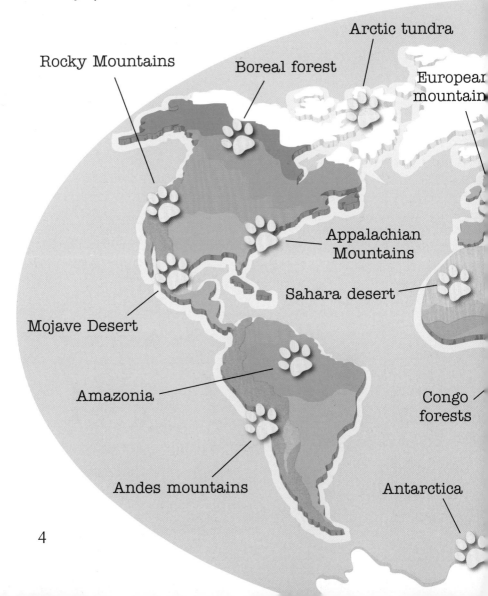

Arctic tundra

Rocky Mountains

Boreal forest

European mountain

Appalachian Mountains

Sahara desert

Mojave Desert

Amazonia

Congo forests

Andes mountains

Antarctica

Most of the wilderness areas are found in places where few people live – this is why they haven't been changed by human action. Many of them are now threatened by expanding human populations.

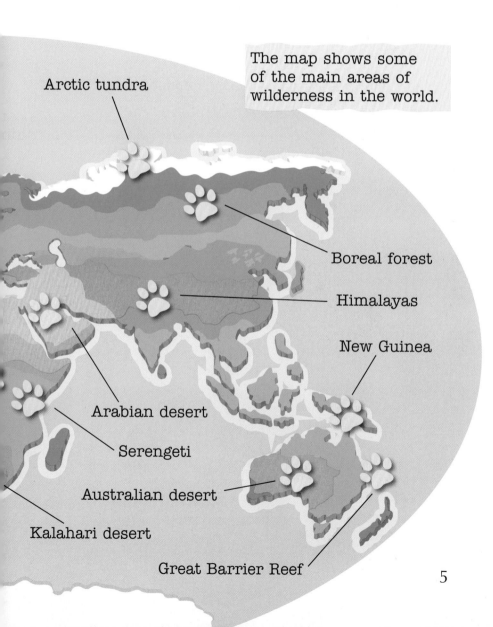

The map shows some of the main areas of wilderness in the world.

Arctic tundra

Boreal forest

Himalayas

New Guinea

Arabian desert

Serengeti

Australian desert

Kalahari desert

Great Barrier Reef

Types of wilderness

There are several types of wilderness, including forest, grassland, desert and wetland. The type of wilderness in an area depends on the climate there.

Forest

Tropical rainforest is found near the **equator**, and has high rainfall and constant warm temperatures. The Amazon rainforest is the largest tropical rainforest on Earth.

conifers in a boreal forest

Amazon rainforest, Brazil

Temperate areas are areas with four different seasons. The forests in these areas mainly contain **deciduous** trees – trees that lose their leaves in autumn. The largest one in Europe is the Bialowieza Forest in Poland.

Boreal forest is found in Asia, the north of Europe and North America, for instance, in Alaska, where it's cold for much of the year. The trees are mainly conifers like pine and spruce, which have needle-shaped leaves and don't lose them in winter.

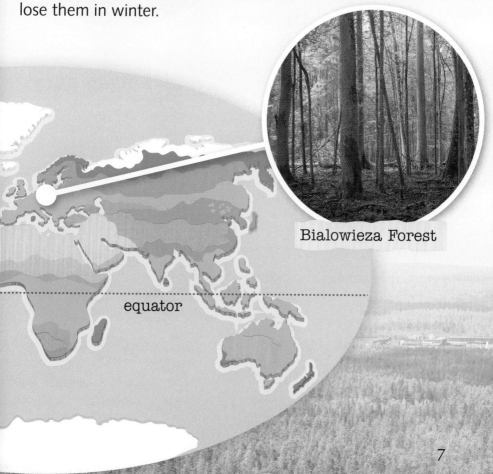

Bialowieza Forest

equator

You don't need trees to make a wilderness. There are other types too.

Grassland

Grasslands have few trees, but lots of grasses and flowers. Some of these grasses can be up to four metres tall. The Serengeti in Tanzania is one of the most famous grassland areas.

the Serengeti

Desert

Deserts are all dry, but not all of them are hot. The Sahara and Namib in Africa are deserts, but so is the Antarctic. Only very specialised species of plant and animal can live in deserts.

WILD FACT
In parts of the Antarctic, it hasn't rained for nearly two million years.

Antarctica

Wetland

Wetlands are areas of **standing water** – marshes, bogs and swamps. The Sundarbans in India and Okavango Delta in Botswana are important wetlands.

Okavango Delta

Sahara desert

Threats to wilderness

Unfortunately, most of the threats to wilderness areas come from human activities.

Logging destroys large areas of tropical rainforest, and large areas of forest are cleared in some places so that oil palm trees can be grown as a **cash crop** instead. Their oil is widely used for cooking, and can also be turned into fuel for vehicles.

logging in the Amazon rainforest

palm oil plantation

Wetlands – especially **peat bogs** – are drained, trees are cleared and the land is ploughed so it can be used for **agriculture**. As wetlands act as a natural sponge by soaking up rainwater, removing them can make flooding in nearby areas more likely.

excavation of a peat bog

As cities expand, wild areas around them are destroyed and replaced by buildings. Roads break up areas of wilderness, making it difficult for animals to move between the areas that are left.

trees are cleared to build a road

Other threats to the wilderness come from drilling to find oil, and **mining**. These destroy the structure of the land itself, leaving scars that can take many years to disappear. We depend on oil to make petrol, diesel and other products. Mining is also needed to obtain coal, metals, salt, gravel, precious stones and many other substances. Air and water **pollution** caused by mining can damage plants, animals, soil and even rocks.

oil field

If people bring plants and animals into an area where they aren't usually found, these **invasive species** may be better at surviving than the **native species**. If this happens, some of the native plant and animal species can die out completely, because they can't compete for things like food and space.

And finally, climate change may alter the conditions that allow some of the most fragile **ecosystems** to exist. If the climate in an area becomes hotter, colder, wetter or drier, the plants and animals which have adapted to live in that area may not be able to cope with the change and become **extinct**.

burning rhododendrons

Why should we preserve wildernesses?

Wildernesses have taken millions of years to develop, and the plants and animals that live there have become **highly adapted**. Many can't live anywhere else.

For instance, orangutans are only found in the rainforests of Borneo and Sumatra, and *Rafflesia arnoldii* – the largest flower on Earth – is only found in the rainforests of Sumatra, Indonesia and Malaysia.

Rafflesia arnoldii

If we lose wilderness areas, there are fewer places for plants and animals to live and less for the animals to eat, so fewer types of plant and animal survive.

It's also important that the wild relatives of the plants we depend on for food still survive in the wild, so that they can be used to improve the crops we grow.

The wilderness can also be a potential source of many new medicines. Important cancer treatments have been developed from

Madagascar periwinkle

the Madagascar periwinkle plant and the Pacific yew tree.

And lastly, getting out into wild places has been shown to be good for people's mental and physical health.

How can we preserve wildernesses?

There are a number of ways we can try to prevent humans causing more damage to wilderness areas. These include:

- using education to make people understand what a wilderness is, why it is important, and what they can do to protect it
- passing laws to limit mining and drilling for oil
- passing laws to prevent logging

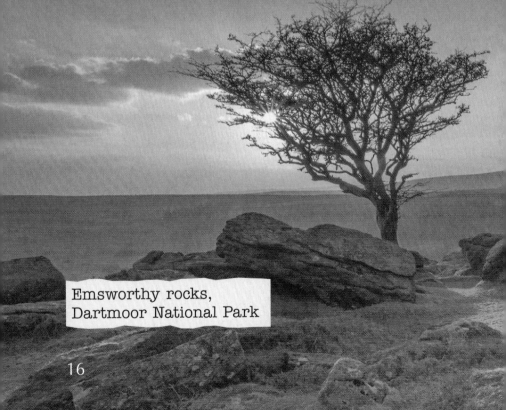

Emsworthy rocks, Dartmoor National Park

- reducing air and water pollution
- limiting human activities in wilderness areas, for instance, banning hunting
- setting up National Parks.

Making National Parks is one of the most effective ways of protecting wilderness areas.

children at Rye Meads learning about wetlands

What is a National Park?

National Parks exist all over the world. They are areas which are preserved in their wild state to protect the landscape and the animals, plants and people who live in them. Almost all of them are open to visitors.

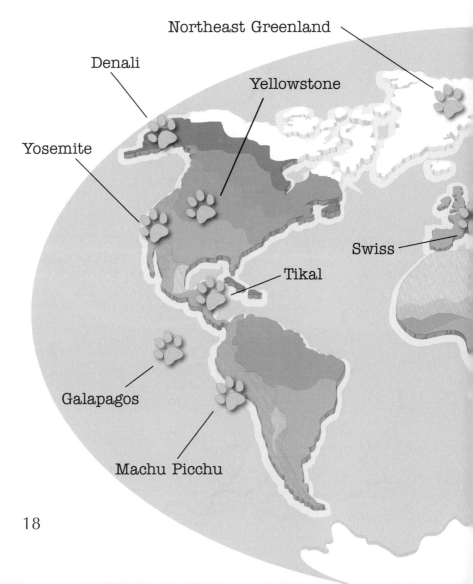

Northeast Greenland

Denali

Yellowstone

Yosemite

Swiss

Tikal

Galapagos

Machu Picchu

Most of them are large areas that haven't been altered very much by human activity. They usually contain animals, plants and landscapes which are important, rare, beautiful or educational. They are protected by the laws of the countries they are in.

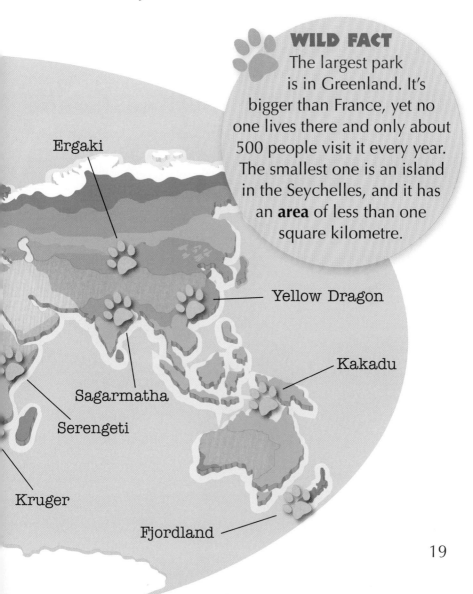

WILD FACT
The largest park is in Greenland. It's bigger than France, yet no one lives there and only about 500 people visit it every year. The smallest one is an island in the Seychelles, and it has an **area** of less than one square kilometre.

Ergaki

Yellow Dragon

Kakadu

Sagarmatha

Serengeti

Kruger

Fjordland

19

Yellowstone – the first National Park

The first National Park to be created was Yellowstone, which covers parts of Wyoming, Montana and Idaho in the US. It became a National Park in 1872.

WILD FACT
Yellowstone has thousands of small **earthquakes** every year. The largest one in the last century was in 1959. It killed 28 people and created a new lake, named Earthquake Lake.

Explorers reported the presence of **geysers** and other unusual features in the 1860s and suggested that the area should be protected and turned into a public park. In 1872, the US president signed the law that made Yellowstone a National Park, so that people could enjoy it forever. However, this meant Native American communities could no longer use the area, and local people were unhappy because they thought it would be difficult to make a living if mining, hunting and logging were forbidden in the park.

More about Yellowstone

Yellowstone has over 1,700 species of plant. At least one – the Yellowstone sand verbena – is found nowhere else. It also has one of the biggest **petrified forests** in the world.

petrified trees

Over 60 species of mammal live in the park, including bison, black and grizzly bears, grey wolves, coyote and mountain lions. Bison are protected while they're in the park, but unfortunately they're often killed if they wander outside, by ranchers who worry they'll pass on diseases to their cattle.

bison

grizzly bears

Animals that don't usually live in the park can cause problems if they arrive. Bark beetles destroy the pine trees, and lake trout that were released years ago in some of the lakes eat the cutthroat trout that really belong there.

There are hundreds of geysers in Yellowstone. The best known is Old Faithful, which spouts water every one to two hours. The geysers, **hot springs** and earthquakes are because Yellowstone sits on top of a **supervolcano**, but it's thousands of years since the last big volcanic eruption.

Old Faithful

coyote

John Muir

John Muir was born in
Scotland in 1838 and
moved with his family to
America when he was 11.
He became fascinated
by the natural world and
was one of the first people to
argue that wilderness areas should
be preserved. When he moved to California, he fell in
love with the Yosemite wilderness, built a log cabin and
lived there. He realised the landscape had been shaped by
glaciers during the ice ages, and eventually managed to
persuade other people he was right.

Yosemite Valley has been carved
out by the Merced River.

He wrote magazine articles in 1889 arguing that Yosemite should become a National Park, and in 1890, the US government took his advice. He also helped set up the Sequoia National Park and founded the Sierra Club, which was set up to "explore, enjoy, and protect the wild places of the earth". The club still exists and campaigns on environmental issues. John Muir probably did more than any other person to persuade governments to protect wilderness and is known as the "Father of National Parks".

GLACIERS

Glaciers are huge masses of ice that flow like very slow rivers. They are leftovers from the last ice age. Their weight and movement scrape away layers of rock beneath them as they flow, producing deep valleys.

Alibeksky glacier, Russia

Yosemite

Yosemite is in California. It's famous for its wild landscapes and contains many spectacular waterfalls. Much of the landscape was created by glaciers moving across it and there are still some small glaciers in the park. Animals include black bears, cougars and spotted owls. The most famous plants in Yosemite are the giant sequoia trees, also known as redwoods. They can be more than 2,000 years old and over 80 metres tall. Sequoias are only found in California.

spotted owl

cougar

WILD FACT
The biggest sequoia in Yosemite is the General Sherman Tree, which is 83 metres high and 11 metres in diameter.

27

Managing Yosemite

With more and more visitors trying to reach Yosemite, traffic jams, and pollution caused by chemicals and dirt in car exhaust fumes have become a problem. Animals in the park are in danger from traffic, both from the pollution it brings and the chance of being hit by a car. To combat this, the park has introduced electric buses, which don't give off exhaust fumes, and encourages people to park their cars at the edge of the park and use these instead.

Black bears can be a problem when tourists leave food lying around, as this attracts the bears – sometimes they even break into cars. It's important that bears don't come into contact with people in case they attack them. This is important for the bears too, because if they become aggressive, they have to be shot.

a warning sign in Yosemite

Sequoias are being damaged by air pollution, and it's difficult for new ones to grow – the seeds will only start to grow in soil where there's been a fire, so controlled fires are set to help them. Wildfires, on the other hand, can cause huge damage.

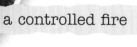

a controlled fire

Sagarmatha

Sagarmatha is in Nepal and borders China. Mount Everest (called Mount Sagarmatha in Nepali) sits on the border and is the world's highest mountain. The rare animals found there include snow leopards and red pandas. Only 3% of the park is forest, and this is threatened by demand for firewood. About 6,000 **Sherpas** live within the park. They respect all forms of life, and this has been very important in conserving the area's wildlife. The Nepalese Army also helps to protect the park and its wildlife.

snow leopard

Many tourists want to visit the area, or even climb Everest. The huge increase in visitors has improved standards of living for the Sherpas, but has also caused problems. Visitors want somewhere to stay, so hotels and lodges are built. They use energy and produce rubbish – and the disposal of rubbish is a real problem in this remote area. Everest itself is littered with equipment left behind by climbing parties. All the organisations involved in looking after Sagarmatha are trying to find solutions to these problems.

Sherpas collecting litter

The Great Barrier Reef

The Great Barrier Reef, off the coast of Australia, is the biggest coral reef system in the world and contains about 10% of all coral reefs. It's home to thousands of species of animals including dugongs, 14 species of sea snake, six species of turtle and over 1,500 species of fish. Many of these species are **endangered** and the reef is an important habitat for them.

a dugong

CORAL REEFS

Coral reefs are rock-like ridges in the sea. They are made from the skeletons of tiny coral animals and take up to 10,000 years to form. The Great Barrier Reef is probably about 20,000 years old.

It's an important area for scientists studying marine life, and a popular destination for tourists, especially divers. There's also a fishing industry. The park authority manages the reef so that all these things can take place, while still protecting the reef and its wildlife.

However, the reef is threatened by climate change and there's evidence that increased sea temperatures can cause the coral to die. It's also threatened by the crown-of-thorns starfish, which can eat the coral faster than it can grow. The starfish are destroyed to protect the coral.

crown-of-thorns starfish

33

National Parks in the UK

There are 15 National Parks in the UK. They are looked after by National Park authority staff and volunteers. Other organisations like the National Trust and the Forestry Commission own land in some of the parks and are involved in looking after them.

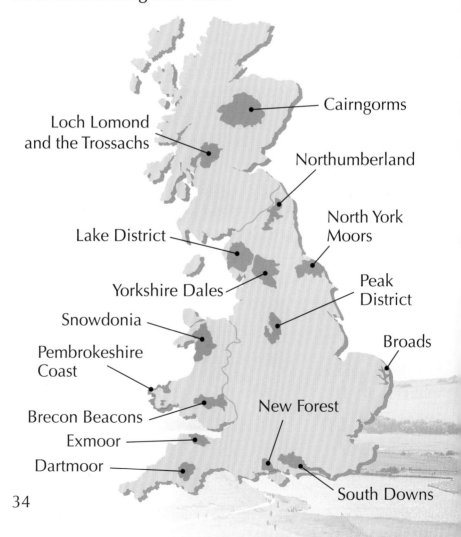

Cairngorms

Loch Lomond and the Trossachs

Northumberland

North York Moors

Lake District

Yorkshire Dales

Peak District

Snowdonia

Broads

Pembrokeshire Coast

Brecon Beacons

New Forest

Exmoor

Dartmoor

South Downs

The first park to be established was the Peak District, in 1951, and the most recent was the South Downs, in 2010.

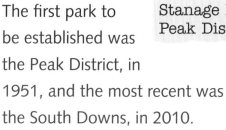
Stanage Edge, Peak District

Altogether, National Parks cover almost 10% of England, 20% of Wales and 7% of Scotland. The largest park is the Cairngorms in Scotland, and the smallest is the Norfolk and Suffolk Broads.

Some National Parks have towns and villages in them, and there are often strict rules about building in these areas so that they keep their traditional character.

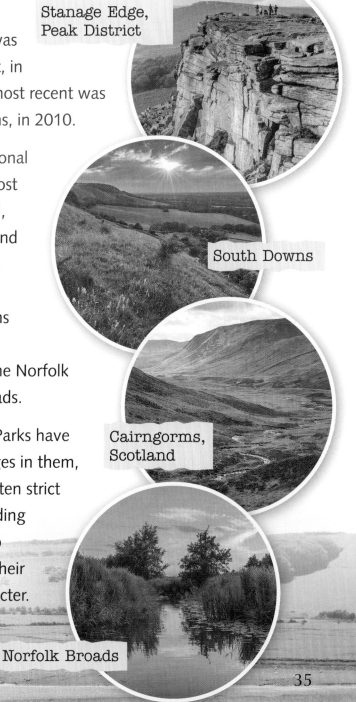
South Downs

Cairngorms, Scotland

Norfolk Broads

The Lake District

The landscape of the Lake District was created by glaciers over the last two million years. They left long valleys, many of which became lakes, and mountains known as "fells". There are about 210 fells and 16 lakes. All the land in England higher than 3,000 metres is in the Lake District, including Scafell Pike, England's highest mountain.

WILD FACT
Only one stretch of water in the Lake District is called a lake – Bassenthwaite Lake. The others are called "meres" – like Buttermere – or "waters" – like Ullswater.

The Lake District provides a home for ospreys, red squirrels and fell ponies, and patches of uncommon **carnivorous** plants called sundew and butterwort.

Almost 41,000 people live in the Lake District, and many of them are involved in farming, especially sheep farming and forestry work. It is the most visited National Park in the UK.

osprey

red squirrel

fell pony

sundew

Managing the Lake District

Most National Parks are wildernesses, and we want them to stay that way, but at the same time, it's important that people visit them as this is a major source of income to help with their upkeep. Lots of people live within National Parks, and they need houses, jobs, shops, schools and roads.

In the Lake District, erosion of paths is a big problem because so many people go walking there. Paths are repaired with local stone, and plants are introduced along the sides of the paths to stabilise the soil.

WILD FACT
In boggy areas, sheep's wool is used as a base layer in path repairs.

Traffic is another problem. So many people visit the Lake District, in addition to the people who live there, that the narrow roads get very busy, and this brings pollution problems.

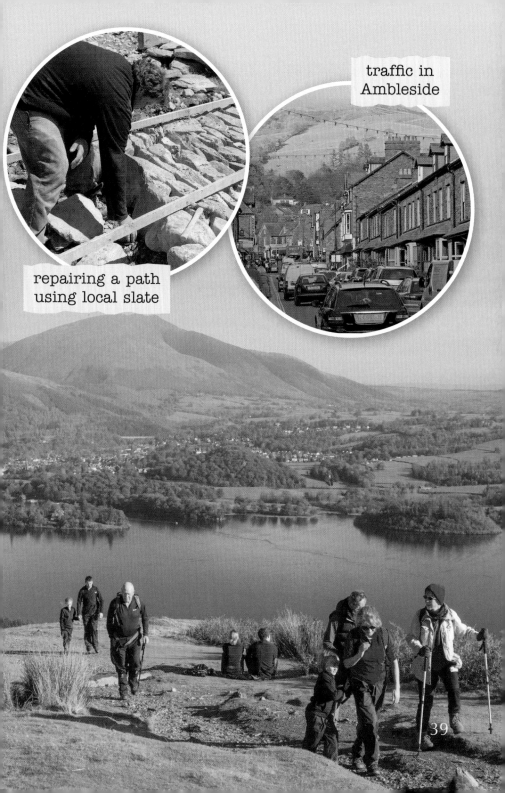

repairing a path
using local slate

traffic in
Ambleside

The Broads

The Norfolk and Suffolk Broads is an unusual National Park, because it is a man-made landscape, not a wilderness. In the Middle Ages, people dug up peat bogs and used the dried peat as fuel for fires. Rising sea levels flooded the holes left where peat had been dug out, and systems of lakes, marshes, reed beds and woodland developed.

It's been a popular holiday destination since the 19th century, with many visitors hiring boats. The waves caused by the boats can damage the river banks, however, so there is a strict speed limit.

The Broads is Britain's biggest wetland area and provides a home for birds like bitterns and marsh harriers, and many insects, including the Norfolk hawker, a rare dragonfly.

Norfolk hawker dragonfly

The Broads are threatened by fertiliser pollution from farming, which can kill animals and plants in the water and also causes sludge to build up, and by invasive species like the Himalayan balsam plant and the signal crayfish. These can survive better than native plants and animals, which may die out as a result.

signal crayfish

Conclusion

In the last few hundred years, we've stopped thinking of wilderness as something to avoid and be afraid of, and have realised that it's precious and **irreplaceable**. Unfortunately, humans are the biggest threat to wilderness areas, and we have a great responsibility to look after the ones still left.

National Parks worldwide are doing a great deal to help with this, but they depend on people to make them work – people who run the organisations that look after the parks, staff who work in them, volunteers who help with projects, and the people who live and work in villages and towns within them. And of course, they need visitors, who bring in the money that allows many of the parks to function, but can also bring problems.

We can all help to preserve our wonderful wildernesses – and if we don't, they'll soon be gone forever.

Glossary

agriculture	farming
area	size of a surface
carnivorous	meat-eating
cash crop	plants that can be grown and sold to make money
deciduous	trees that shed their leaves in autumn
earthquakes	sudden shakings of the earth, as a result of moving continental plates or volcanic activity
ecosystems	communities of living and non-living things in specific areas
endangered	under threat; in danger
equator	an imaginary line around the middle of the earth
extinct	have died out completely
geysers	boiling springs of water that shoot out of the ground
highly adapted	well-suited to the place they live
hot springs	springs of hot (sometimes boiling) water that come from underground, heated by the molten rock in volcanic areas
invasive species	animals or plants that are not natural to a specific area
irreplaceable	impossible to replace or put back
logging	cutting down trees to use their wood
mining	the extraction of material from the earth
native species	the plants and animals that normally live in an area
peat bogs	wetland areas made up of dead plants, often moss

petrified forests   forests of trees that have become fossilised, turning them into stone

pollution   introduction of natural or unnatural things into an environment that can have a harmful effect

Sherpas   Nepalese people who are Buddhists

significantly   in a way that is important enough to have an effect

standing water   non-flowing water

supervolcano   a huge volcano

Index

Different types of wilderness

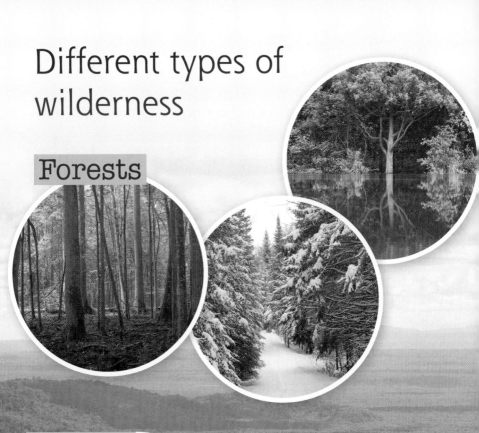

Forests

Marine

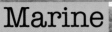

Grassland

Wetland

Desert

Mountains

47

 Ideas for reading

Written by Clare Dowdall, PhD
Lecturer and Primary Literacy Consultant

Reading objectives:
- read books that are structured in different ways
- ask questions to improve understanding
- make predictions from details stated and implied
- retrieve and record information from non-fiction

Spoken language objectives:
- use spoken language to develop understanding through speculating, hypothesising, imagining and exploring ideas

Curriculum links: Science – living things and their habitats
Geography – geographical skills and fieldwork

Resources: ICT, atlas

Build a context for reading
- Ask children to describe the wildest or most remote place on Earth that they have visited or know about.
- Look at the cover of the book and read the title. Ask children to suggest what they think a wilderness is. Notice the clue from the word "wild" in wilderness.
- Read the blurb and check that children understand the meaning of the word "preserve". Discuss why we might need to preserve the world's wilderness areas.

Understand and apply reading strategies
- Turn to the contents and read through the first seven headings. Ask children to either raise a question or make a prediction about the content in these chapters.
- Read pp2–5 aloud. Model how to wonder as you read by answering your own questions, making predictions and raising new questions, e.g. *So a wilderness is a wild, unchanged place ...*